CRANK IT!

CRANK IT!

A PLAYBOOK

for

SUCCEEDING

IN BUSINESS

and

LIFE

DAVE LAMONT

LIONCREST

PUBLISHING

CRANK IT!

A Playbook for Succeeding in Business and Life

FIRST EDITION

ISBN   978-1-5445-4393-2   *Hardcover*
      978-1-5445-4392-5   *Paperback*
      978-1-5445-4391-8   *Ebook*
      978-1-5445-4394-9   *Audiobook*

To my Brother Douglas J. Lamont

CONTENTS

INTRODUCTION

One bright sunny day in the middle of summer, two boats sat in the marina. One was a $2 million yacht, decked out with all the latest gadgets. The other was an $80,000 Mastercraft—a comfortable boat, but certainly nothing luxurious.

Two people boarded the $2 million yacht, while ten people boarded the $80,000 Mastercraft—and another ten people stood on the dock waiting for a chance to join in the fun.

Which owner was actually successful?

Success and money are two different things. Sure, they overlap in many cases, but having enough money to buy a state-of-the-art yacht doesn't automatically mean you're successful. Passion, charisma, self-discipline, kindness—these qualities define true success. They make you the type of person people want to follow, no matter what kind of boat you own.

If you think the guy with the $2 million yacht is the more successful of the two, then maybe this book isn't for you. But if you want to learn how to be the person with a waiting list—someone who builds relationships, serves others, and leads by example—read on.

THANK YOU, MOM AND DAD

So much of the success I have today started with my upbringing. I was born and raised in Calgary, Alberta, Canada, and both of my parents pushed me hard to learn and grow.

My mother was a social worker, which was a great help to me growing up. As a child, I struggled with a learning disability—I learned visually, not auditorily, but most teachers instructed through lectures. Back in the mid-1980s, learning disabilities like mine were not as widely recognized, but my mom was determined to not let this hold me back. She did lengthy research, and when I was in grade five, she enrolled me into the Calgary Academy, where I received the assistance I needed. This was a defining moment in my life—the first time I realized I could do anything with help and hard work.

My father, whom we called Poppy, was a firm but fair man—sometimes a little too firm, but his strictness helped mold me nonetheless. If I mowed the lawn and it wasn't cut just right, he would come outside and say, "No, no, no, David. *This* is how it's done." If I missed a spot while shoveling the walk, he'd send me back out to fix it. He demanded perfection, which has carried me far in life.

My dad owned a commercial refrigeration business and worked no less than six days a week. He often took me with him on Saturdays, so I saw firsthand what hard work looked like. Later in life, he was quite successful, and the connection between his work ethic and his success was not lost on me.

My older brother, Doug, and I were great friends growing up, and we still are to this day. Like me, he was pushed, in a good way, to work hard and do what's right. Doug now owns the commercial refrigeration company started by our father, and over the past ten-plus years he has enjoyed record numbers.

After my learning disability was corrected, school became much easier and I did fairly well in high school—not *exactly* straight As, but good enough to earn an advanced high school diploma.

During high school, I worked at Safeway as a utility clerk, an excellent job for a seventeen-year-old—it came with local 401 union benefits, and $16.02 an hour wasn't bad back then. I had no intentions of going to university. My mother, again caring about my education, said to me one day, "Why not just go and try a semester? If you don't like it, quit; you'll at least be able to say you tried and didn't want to."

She made a good point, and since my brother was already a student at the University of Montana (Go Griz, Go!), I gave it a try. Turns out Mom nailed it again. Mothers do know best.

Interestingly, I found that university was even easier than high school, mainly because I found a love for business. Having a passion for what I was learning made a huge difference. Now I studied what I wanted to, not what I had to. Like the old saying goes, "Find a job you enjoy doing, and you will never have to work a day in your life." School became fun, and I loved it. Bonus:

I made the varsity club hockey team and met some great people. We even won a few games.

It helped that I developed good reading and writing skills when I was younger, again thanks to my mom. When I was in grade school, she'd say, "Davey, it doesn't matter what you're reading; if you're reading, you're learning."

She was right. As a kid, I read muscle car magazines; as a university student, it was business books. Because of this grounding, I excelled. One semester I took seven courses totaling twenty-one credits and wound up with a 3.4 GPA—pretty good for this guy.

I believe my interest and love of business came from my father, who had a finance degree from the University of Montana. As a businessman, he constantly had people coming in from Toronto, Chicago, and many other cities, and he would invite them over for dinner. The best part was that he wanted Doug and me to join them at the table so we could listen to their conversation. I'll never forget that—being ten years old and watching my father talk business and make deals right there in our dining room. I'd stay up till midnight captivated by the discussion, soaking it all in.

I didn't know it at the time, but my father was training me. They weren't structured lessons, more like learning by immersion—observing his interactions with people and how he approached different characters and situations.

Because of these lessons, I knew what I wanted to study when I enrolled in university. I signed up for the business marketing program, and the rest is history.

HARD WORK + RISK-TAKING = SUCCESS

I graduated from the University of Montana in December of 1994 and started work with Chrysler Corporation early the next year as the district manager of the regional offices for western Canada. When I got the job, you'd have thought I won the lottery. I was a twenty-three-year-old with a thousand-dollar-a-week salary, a company car (fuel included), and an expense account—I was flying high.

But I didn't let it go to my head. I worked hard, and three years later I received a promotion to district manager for the whole province of British Columbia. So, off I went to the head office in Vancouver, where I continued to crank it—and started dreaming big. Really big. I decided I wanted to own my own dealership.

One day I decided to share my dream with Rick Moore, the owner of the Maple Ridge Chrysler dealership in British Columbia. The conversation went something like this:

"Hey, Rick. I've been looking at this Toyota dealership I would like to buy."

Without skipping a beat, Rick said, "Lamont, you're crazy. You're gonna get killed. You can't go from corporate to retail without being a sales manager. You need some experience."

I knew he was right.

"Why don't you come to my Maple Ridge dealership as a sales manager," Rick continued. "You've got the corporate experience and you know your stuff. It'd be great for you."

I told him I'd sleep on it, and after we hung up, I went to my dad and my brother for advice.

"Davey, are you crazy?!" shouted my dad. My mom and brother were right there with him.

"You're making, what, a hundred and a half in your twenties?" my dad continued. "You have a company car *and* an expense account? What about your pension?"

He had a valid point. I had a solid corporate job, a substantial paycheck, and a secure future. I had seven years' experience in corporate, and after twenty I would have a pension for life.

And I was talking about risking it all.

After considering Rick's offer and my family's advice, I decided to go for it. I had no wife and kids, I was young and motivated, and this was a stepping stone to the goal of owning my own dealership. It was a scary move with zero guarantees, but I knew I had to take the risk and jump into the deep end.

Looking back now, that was obviously the right move, but at the time I often felt like I was in way over my head—I had jumped straight into a sales manager position without any sales experience. But I was already in the water at that point, so I figured I might as well swim. With help from another sales manager named Steve Phillips and general manager Ian Speckman, I learned the ropes. Soon sales became easier, and I started to enjoy it.

No, I more than enjoyed it. I loved it! I would work from eight in the morning till nine at night and come home pumped with adrenaline because the dealership had sold twenty cars in one day. Just like in university, I had found something I was passionate about and I cranked it.

Taking that chance launched me into a new sphere of possibility. In 2002, after two years at Maple Ridge, I received a call from Mike Tarp, the owner of Renfrew Chrysler in Calgary, who offered me a position as general sales manager. Over the next year and a half, I brought the dealership's sales up so much that Renfrew became the number one dealership in Calgary. I moved on to general manager positions at a couple of other dealerships, and then in 2006 I was presented with the golden opportunity I had been working toward: the chance to own my own store (I'll save the details on that for a later chapter).

I was thirty-four when I officially took over the Renfrew Store in 2008—one of the youngest principal owners and general managers for a North American Chrysler that wasn't family or group owned. I still work six days a week, and I still love my job, every single day.

TIME TO GIVE BACK

My success is not my own. I would never have reached where I am today without my mother correcting my learning disability, my father pushing me to perfection and involving me in his world, my teachers providing a business foundation and life skills, Rick Moore offering advice, Steven Philips taking me under his wing, Mike Tarp demonstrating leadership, and the help of a host of others I haven't mentioned. I am the sum of hundreds of people's guidance and mentorships.

Now it's my turn to give back.

I know what it's like to just be starting out. The world of opportunity is so vast that sometimes you don't even know what to ask. I want to offer my experiences of success and failure to help orient you on your journey, just as others did for me. You are already headed in the right direction by reading this book—you know that a little help never hurts anyone.

The only stupid question is the question you don't ask, and this book will answer many. I'll help you think through your plans for your education and career path, the importance of hard work and calculated risk, and the value of organization both personally and professionally. Most importantly, perhaps, I'll help you become the kind of person other people want on their team and, someday, as their coach.

Consider this your inspirational guidebook to help you navigate the path to success. If I can help you make your parents proud and make you proud of yourself, I'm a happy man. I've practiced "paying it forward" all my life in business and in my personal relationships, and I want to do the same with this book. I hope that you gain something from my experience and become more successful than me—one day passing down what you've learned, just like my mentors did from their mentors.

FOR THE DREAMERS AND THE GRINDERS

This book is for those who didn't wake up as a trust fund baby. It's for those who want to make their pipe dream into a feasible reality. It's for those who are ready to be led, who are teachable, and who want actionable steps to achieve their goals. It's for people who believe their career dream can truly happen and are willing to put in the hard work to get there.

At the same time, this book is not a "Guaranteed Way to Make Millions" hype fest. You've heard it before: there are no guarantees in life. But this book will give you the resources, inspiration, and plans to create opportunities for yourself.

Sadly, I've had to help friends in their fifties declutter their life because they made all the wrong choices in their twenties and thirties. They wake up middle-aged, unpassionate, and miserable. I don't want that to happen to anyone else.

Even so, if you are older and find yourself unsatisfied, this book can show you how to change your circumstances, how to become who you want to be, how to go from victim to victor. Warren Buffet made 98 percent of his net worth after fifty years of age, so it's not too late. Young or old, climbing the corporate ladder or stepping out into retail, the principles laid down in this book will help you succeed in business and in life.

If a kid with a learning disability can work his way up to owning one of the top-ten most profitable dealerships in Canada, you can reach your business goals, too. You can be successful. You have what it takes.

We'll start with the importance of being the kind of person people want on their team.

CHAPTER 1

BE A TEAM PLAYER

When I first started working for Chrysler, I was twenty-three years old while most of my teammates were over *fifty*. From the beginning I knew that even though it seemed like I didn't have much in common with these guys, I couldn't stand awkwardly in the corner at corporate events. I had to find a way to fit in.

Within a week or so, I learned that a group regularly went next door to a local pub after work. One of those people was the man I reported to, Owen, who was twenty-five years older than me.

"Hey, Owen," I said at work one day. "Do you know if the pub next door has VLTs? I used to play in Montana."

"As a matter of fact they do," Owen replied. "Want to go play after work?"

Of course, I already knew the pub had VLTs, or video lottery terminals, and I already knew that Owen played them. I used this knowledge to make a connection, to invite myself into his interests without outright inviting myself, and we ended up hitting it off in a big way.

When 5:30 rolled around that day, Owen and I walked to the pub, had some drinks, and then played some VLTs. As we played, we talked. I asked what brought him to Chrysler Corporation, how long he had worked there, and what got him interested in that kind of work. I was genuinely interested in his career path, and that day sparked a close working relationship that lasted for years.

If you think I was being a brownnoser, you're wrong. Friendships are made by choosing to be genuinely interested in people. You have to work on your relationships like you do your job or business. To be able to interact with anyone is a valuable—and learnable—skill, one that shows you want to be on the team.

In this chapter we'll talk about the most important attributes and attitudes you can develop to show that you're a team player.

FIND YOUR PASSION

To me, passion is one of the most important attributes you can have in business. It's a key element of success, individually and as a team. But what is passion, really?

Passion is being interested in and consumed with what you're doing, to the point where you think about it even when you're not getting paid to do so. When you are motivated to plan and strategize in your off time, you've found your passion. Without passion, you're just another number looking for a paycheck.

Passionate people are the ones who expand, grow, and get excited about their work. They find joy in excelling; just take a look at those who are extremely successful. One of my friends is now seventy years old and worth $500 million, but he wants to reach

$1 billion before he dies—not because he loves money, but because he loves his business and wants to make it better. He's passionate about business and figuring out what it takes to be the best. He didn't get to that level by working for a paycheck. He poured an immense amount of effort into his work. It's passion that makes those sixty-, seventy-, *eighty*-hour weeks easier and worthwhile.

I don't have to go to work—I *get* to go to work. Passion makes all the difference in how I approach each day. If you love what you do, you will put in more effort. You'll be more conscientious. You'll strive for excellence. You'll be a better team player because you're constantly thinking of ways to improve business for everyone. And as a result, money usually follows. But passion comes first, not the other way around.

HOW TO FIND YOUR PASSION

It's not always easy to find your passion. Sometimes *finding* your passion has to *be* your passion; the process often comes with blood, sweat, and tears. You need to try something out fully before making a decision on whether or not you like it.

The best place to start is to think about what you're already interested in and act on it. I knew I loved cars, so I started in the automotive industry. My mom loved helping people, so she became a social worker. For you, it might be real estate, law, finances, construction, clothing, restaurants—you can turn anything you love into a career. Take time to sit and think about what gives you joy. Then think about how you can incorporate this passion into your business or career.

Whether you're an entrepreneur, CEO, salesperson, or something entirely different, passion is the key to getting the most out of business, work, and life. If you're going to do something, do something you like. Don't waste your time.

BE SELF-DISCIPLINED

Self-disciplined people know how to do what they need to do to get the job done excellently. If the meeting is at 8:00, they show up at 7:50 to make sure they're on time. If they're under a deadline, they'll miss an after-hours party or give up tickets to a pro sports game if needed to finish the work. If they have an early morning meeting, the night before, they'll lay out clothes and do whatever else they need to do to get out the door on time. They'll wake up every day as if they have an interview: dressed in their best, shoes shined, wearing a positive attitude. It may not be easy to do every day, but self-disciplined people can make it happen.

When I started at Chrysler Corporation, I was told that the first person came in around 6:30 a.m. I was shocked! So, I made it my goal to arrive by 6:00. It was not easy, but it certainly paid dividends. When I traveled, I would hit the road on Sunday so I could get to the hotel and be ready to make a dealership call Monday morning. I sacrificed half of my weekend, but my teammates took note.

BE POLITE, BUT SPEAK YOUR MIND

Balance is key here. Be polite and treat others with respect, but don't be a pushover either. Don't be afraid to speak up when you think something is wrong. I respect people all the more when they stand up to the boss and politely tell me when I'm off. I respect that they are willing to take the risk. Speaking your mind in a clear, considerate manner makes a strong statement of your strength of character to your peers and superiors.

Respect goes a long way in business relationships and friendships, as well as in meeting someone for the first time. If you treat everyone with the same respect—whether they are the CEO or your peer—you will be treated the same way 99 percent of the time. The 1 percent who don't reciprocate? You probably don't want them in your life anyway.

One final note: the words *please* and *thank you* go a long way in every business relationship. I certainly notice the people who don't speak this way, and the ones who do stand out in a positive way.

BE A GOOD PERSON

Here's a basic rule: be a good person. Help people without expecting anything in return. Be kind. Do the right thing.

Back in my time at corporate, there was a guy who was having trouble with his expense account. I took the time to teach him how to manage it properly. Though it wasn't my goal, this act ingratiated me with the team in a large way. Likewise, when I saw that a certain dealership was not performing to the level it should be, I went above and beyond to help them. Not for recognition but to be a good person. Again, if you want to be on the team, *be a team player.*

Think about it this way: if you're being interviewed and you have the same qualifications as the next person, what's one thing that might set you apart? Being a good person. If you can meet the requirements of the position *and* be a joy to work with, you stand a good chance of being hired.

LISTEN

"How was your weekend?" "Did you go out for dinner after work on Saturday?" I ask my employees these types of questions often, not just as a pleasantry but because I'm interested in their lives. I want my workers to know they're not just a number and that I really care for them, their families, and even their pets.

Whether you're asking questions to get to know people or to understand a situation at work, really listen to the response. Taking notes shows interest, and it can also help you remember the information. Repeat back what you hear to make sure you comprehend the point. Other ways to show the person you're engaged in the conversation: make eye contact, nod, and do not interrupt; if you do, make sure to apologize. Also remember that body language is important. For example, crossing your arms when you're talking to people can come across as standoffish. Finally, as you listen, try not to judge the person's point as right or wrong. Just listen. This shows that you value the person and their perspective, even if you don't agree with it.

HAVE A POSITIVE ATTITUDE

"If you believe you can, you will." I live by this statement. There's nothing I can't achieve if I set my mind to it—within reason, of course (this Canadian won't be running the Oval Office any time soon). As a young man, I believed I would own a dealership and now I do.

To get the most out of life, you have to cast aside all negative thinking; it holds you back. When you experience hardship, you can respond one of two ways: get depressed or get motivated. You can choose to be negative and give up, or you can be positive and look at obstacles as opportunities for growth. You can stop and turn around at a roadblock, or simply view it as a sign that you're headed in the right direction.

Negative people complain about everything: their car, their bills, their job, you name it. The issue is with how they frame their world—*their perspective*. If you have this issue, you need to shift your view and start reframing what you see. For example, if today you are bothered because you have to go to work, pick up the laundry, and stop by the gas pump, stop and reframe: "I have a job. I have clothes. I have a car." The same principle applies to your problems. You don't have roadblocks; you have *challenges*. You have direction signs, not stop signs.

Here's another mindset shift to help you stay positive: failure doesn't exist; learning does. Remember what Thomas Edison said when he was questioned about his failures in inventing the light bulb? "I have not failed. I've just found ten thousand ways that won't work."

Problems, roadblocks, and failures cause people to beat themselves up, complain, and quit because they don't see the control they have. Success doesn't come from magic or luck; it comes from *choosing* to approach life with a positive, can-do attitude, no matter what happens. When my jacket was stolen at a Calgary Flames game, I could have gotten angry and complained, but I didn't. Instead I said, "Oh good, I needed a new one. I hope the guy really needed it." I chose to view the situation differently.

This simple mindset shift of turning these day-to-day issues into challenges to conquer makes all the difference. It has led to my success and it can do the same for you. Who do you think people want on their team—the negative complainer or the positive problem solver?

SERVE OTHERS

On an international flight back to Calgary many years ago, my mom received the customs declaration form and started filling it out. Then she looked around and realized there were several people struggling to understand the form because English wasn't their first language. Being the social worker that she is, my mom got out of her seat and walked up and down the aisle helping these people fill out their forms. Her fellow passengers were so grateful that they wanted to buy her a cup of coffee after they deplaned. She declined, because she was more concerned about helping them find baggage claim and retrieve their luggage.

That is what serving others looks like.

So many people nowadays focus on helping others so they can get something in return. That's not true service. Serving others means being aware of others. Do they need something? Is there a way you can help in the moment, no matter how simple? It's not a push-and-pull type thing or an "I'll do this for you but you need to do this for me" agreement.

Something to keep in mind for down the road: good leaders are servants. They help without looking for anything in return. One of my employees wanted to buy a house and I lent her $30,000 interest-free, with a monthly payment on the principal. I didn't want to make money off of her; I just wanted to help. If I see an elderly customer struggling at the coffee station, I'll go and pour a cup for them, not because I want money, but just to serve and be kind.

In a team setting, serving others makes you quite valuable. It shows you recognize that you're part of a group, not just an individual focusing on himself.

DRESS FOR SUCCESS

That old saying "dress for success" is still true in the modern age. Starting out, I wore a suit and tie seven days a week: six days on the lot and the seventh at church. Make much of your appearance by presenting yourself well, and people will welcome you more readily.

FOUNDATION OF SUCCESS

No matter where you work or what business path you pursue, corporate or retail, you will most likely be part of a team. Be the kind of person others want on their team, and you'll create the foundation of success now and in the future.

One of the most important characteristics in any player is coachability. No matter where you are in life and in business, always be learning.

ALWAYS BE LEARNING

In 2006, I enrolled in the National Automobile Dealers Association (NADA) course: a six-week class that increases one's knowledge of the car business. It was not easy by any means but definitely worthwhile. I took the course because I wanted to upgrade my skills and add something nice to my résumé. Plus, I needed the course if I wanted to own a dealership down the road.

Now I send my employees through the same program so they'll know all of the departments—new car, used car, service, parts, and finance—as well as sales. And I make them pay half, not because I'm cheap, but because they need to have some skin in the game. It gives them accountability. You can guess what their passing rate is when they have to pay out of pocket—it's high, to say the least.

The job payoff is amazing. They learn the car business, and we both make more money in the long run. Their investment in building up their skills now allows them to help themselves and those around them.

The same principle applies to you, no matter what industry you work in. If you want to crank it in life and in business, prioritize education, both formal and informal. This chapter will explore the overall benefits and specific topics that can help you no matter where your career takes you.

COLLEGE DEGREE: RECOMMENDED, NOT REQUIRED

Of course you can get a great job without a college degree; people do it every day. But having a degree can open doors that would otherwise remain closed.

There's no way I would be where I am today without a college education. When I was first hired by Chrysler, the company was only accepting applicants with four-year degrees. They didn't even care what degree you held; they just wanted to know that you could start and finish something, and that you could write.

Bottom line: go to college if you can. If you're pursuing your passion, college is an invaluable way to gather skills and acquire knowledge on that passion; that's exactly what I did. In addition, you'll develop general skills that will help you the rest of your life—most notably in writing. Even if you don't formally enroll in university, take college-level courses if you can.

WRITING

Think about the last time you read a well-written letter; it grabbed your attention, right? Whenever someone sends a well-written letter to one of my businesses, it scares me a little, to be honest. It makes me think, "Geez, this guy is smart. He knows what he's talking about. I better pay attention." Compare that to receiving an angry letter, where the person rails at me about this and that, misspelling every other word in the midst of their horrible run-on sentences. The poor quality of their writing undermines their point; I certainly don't take them as seriously.

I have seen the power of writing a well-written letter firsthand. When I sought to gain ownership of Renfrew Chrysler, I had to write a letter to Chrysler Corporation stating my case. I'm convinced that my professional presentation is one of the key factors that won me approval. When I seek financing for new business deals, I take time to lay out my points logically and clearly, and my requests always seem to go to the top of the pile. You can have the same power with your writing.

If your writing isn't up to speed, take a course—online or in person at the local community college. As we'll discuss in later chapters, it's never too late to improve your skills or learn something new.

FINANCE AND MARKETING

If you're going into business, I recommend taking courses in finance and marketing, in addition to writing. You may not want to be a CFO one day, but if you want to climb the corporate ladder or excel in business to any degree, you need to understand the principles of finance. At the very least, you want to be able to ask questions you already know the answers to. Understanding finance helps you understand what's going on beyond your immediate sphere, which makes you a better manager. This is true for all subjects and any position in a company.

Understanding finance allows you to think big. If you understand how loans work, you'll see how a $30 million loan is the same as a $3 million dollar. If the asset you're purchasing creates the income to pay for the loan, the difference is just an extra zero on a computer screen.

Then there's marketing: you need to know how to market because in business nothing happens until you sell something (notice how you started learning *after* I sold you my book). Marketing is all about generating traffic: you need customers to stay in business. But not just any customers: you need to attract quality customers who are loyal.

It's well known in the marketing world that it costs five times more to find a customer than to keep one. To get new customers I have to send out mailers and put ads in the newspaper, on TV and radio, and so on—not cheap. However, I already have a database of twenty thousand customers—that's twenty thousand qualified leads that know my brand and are more likely than random people to buy from my dealership. And I don't have to spend money on expensive marketing campaigns to reach them. I can simply send out an email blast—direct and to the point.

Sales give you the revenue to keep your business afloat, and marketing is a huge part of that, no matter who you are. Sure, Apple may not need to market as much because of their popularity, but you better believe they were marketing in the beginning. That's what helped them make sales and become the industry giant they are today.

Learn how to market and then track your efforts to see what works. It's one of the best skills you can master—corporate or retail.

DRIVE OVER DEGREE

If you are reading this chapter and feel like you can't change your life because you didn't get an education, stop; a lack of a degree isn't the end of the world.

My friend Mike Tarp, the former owner of Renfrew Chrysler, came to Canada from Denmark in 1965 with eighty cents in his pocket. Looking for a sales position, he was turned down at six dealerships because his English was so poor. He took a job cutting carpet and started nagging a Chrysler dealership every day to let him sell cars—a man of true grit. His persistence wore them out and they eventually hired him just so he'd stop asking. Fast-forward a few months, and this immigrant with no money, no education, no experience, and a whole lot o' heart was their top salesman. Fast-forward a few decades, and I was paying him millions for his dealership.

If you can speak English and have more than one dollar, you're already ahead of Mike when he started. If he succeeded, so can you. Mike didn't let his circumstances stop him. He didn't lie down and complain. He got to work—he maximized every opportunity he received. You can believe that man had passion. His lack of education, and all of the other cards stacked against him, was overcome by all the qualities you'll read about in this book—grit, planning, hard work, and more.

Not having an education is not the end—it most certainly wasn't for my friend, God rest his soul. The great news is that you and I have the freedom to develop these qualities and be like Mike.

SLOW QUARTER OVER A QUICK DIME

If you have the opportunity to improve your skills, whether it be attending training, going to college, or taking a course, jump on it. The more skills you have, the more doors will be opened to you. While writing this book, I took a social media course and couldn't have been more excited. It was only a couple of hundred dollars, but I would have paid thousands for the long-term benefits: what I learned from that class can help me start selling three more cars a month. Amazing! Even if only from a return-on-investment standpoint, the class was worth it.

That's exactly what education is: an investment. It's never about the up-front cost; it's about the long-term benefits—the income and life you can have afterward. That NADA course mentioned earlier cost $40,000 per person, but compare that to the money gained from operating a business more effectively. The mindset shift here begins with thinking about future value and asking yourself, "What can I do today that will pay off big time down the road?"

Many middle-aged people tell me that it's not feasible for them to go back to school. I always say, "No problem; you don't have to." Education exists outside of universities and diplomas. There are classes for everything you can imagine, on the internet or in person. The NADA program doesn't give someone a degree, but it seriously upgrades their skills. The same is true of the social media course: I didn't get a degree at the end of the class, but I do have new knowledge. And as we all know, *knowledge is power.*

Ongoing education has nothing to do with age, background, or prerequisites, and everything to do with your initiative and persistence—your keys to being unstoppable. The person who is passionate wants to initiate and continue their learning. The person who wants to achieve their goals is persistent and finds creative ways to get there. To these people, problems are just challenges.

Whether you're thirty years old or sixty, if you have always wanted to start a business but don't know where to begin, go find a course and enroll. Stop by the library and pick up a few books. Read. Self-educate. Pick something and just *start*.

THE POWER OF BOOKS

Speaking of books...I've read hundreds. There is so much knowledge tucked away in those pages. I don't limit myself to industry-specific topics, either. I read a lot of self-help books and am better for it. One of my favorites is *The Power of "I Am"* by Joel Osteen. It showed me how thinking "I can" unlocks all possibilities, like owning a car dealership.

If you aren't into reading like I am, listen to audiobooks. Don't forgo learning just because you don't like the medium. I had a friend once who was having a hard time. I knew he was religious, so I told him to pick up *The Power of "I Am,"* declaring it might help him as it helped me.

"Nah. I'm not really a reader. Thanks."

"Oh, okay! Well, they've got the audio versions too. Give a listen; it could really help you out of where you are right now."

"Eh, maybe."

He had the ability to read/listen and the opportunity to change, but not the drive to do so. The knowledge was there, but the initiative wasn't. What was it someone once said about leading a horse to water?

My friend is the perfect example of where thousands of others are in their lives. They want to change, but they don't *really* want to change. You have to ask yourself a question: "Do I want to be successful?"

If you're happy where you are, no problem. If you want more, then let's get focused. But with either answer, one truth remains: *the day you stop learning is the day you die.*

I live to learn. Life would be no fun if I stopped learning and growing. I hope I'm learning up to the last minute and die book-in-hand. Take this approach to life and business—you'll grow and never stop.

TEACHABILITY TAKES HUMILITY

Never stop learning, even when you reach the top. In fact, I usually see that when a leader gets comfortable, he usually gets fired. When employees see their managers learning new things, they are inspired to do the same. After I announced I was taking the social media course, multiple people signed up to take it with me; others I nicely forced. One older gentleman tried to tell me he was "out of touch with the internet." I said, "Me too! Let's go!"

Being teachable takes humility. Even as the owner, I still admit I don't know *everything*. As an employee, not being teachable is one of the easiest ways to get yourself fired.

My long-time friend Steve MacDonald came to work with me when he was thirty-nine years old. While he had a business degree, he still had to learn *all* the financial side of retail—no small feat. He started at the bottom of the financial department, learned his field, took courses, bettered himself, and now he's running the show. Steve enjoys more freedom, he's happier, he has quadrupled his income and gets satisfaction from his work—all because he was willing to be the newbie and learn.

The great thing about learning is that anyone can do it. It just takes effort. As I've seen, the more effort you put in and the harder you work, the more you create your own luck.

CHAPTER 3

HARD WORK CREATES LUCK

"Hey, you know we have a 2022 Ram 1500 on the lot. It just arrived from the factory, brand new. Want to take a moment while you're waiting for your car and check it out? It's just right over here."

It was 7:30 a.m. and John was the first salesman on the lot once again. He wasn't talking to customers looking to buy. He was seeking out people who came to Renfrew early to drop off their cars for servicing.

John didn't have to do this. He simply saw an opportunity and took advantage of it. He started coming in before everyone else, and as a result, he was selling five additional cars a month.

Is it better to work hard or to be lucky? I say, *why not be both?* John understood this; he understood that hard work creates the opportunity for luck. He saw the early morning customers coming in for oil changes as potential repeat customers and took advantage of it. He made the extra effort and reaped the rewards.

I'll never say, "There's no such thing as luck"—there are just too many things that happen by chance. But I will say that working hard *significantly* betters your chances of being lucky.

Hard work is a key to success no matter what you do. In this chapter, we'll look at the importance of effort, sacrifice, and delayed gratification in creating your own luck.

LUCK HAPPENS FOR A REASON

When people see a highly successful person, they'll often say, "Oh, he's just lucky"—and it certainly appears that way on the surface. What people aren't seeing is the *years* of toil and effort behind a successful person's big break.

That's why I only buy lottery tickets for charity. I don't want to play for myself, win a large sum, and then give someone the chance to attribute my success to luck. It's my hard work and passion over decades that have led to my success. I also don't want other people thinking that winning big is out of their reach. I want them to know they can succeed by working hard and making their own luck. (In case you think I'm bluffing about winning the lottery—it's happened before. In 2010 I won a $600,000 home from the annual children's hospital raffle. I sold the house and gave most of the money back as fast as I could—I certainly didn't need it.)

Sure, some people may be incredibly intelligent and can get away with being lazy, though I haven't seen many examples. What I have seen is the average person with a good work ethic outshining pure intelligence every time. In fact, high intelligence can be a negative trait. Geniuses can get by just with their smarts—no real effort involved, creating laziness. If you ask me, it's better to be of average intelligence.

GRINDERS PLAY TO WIN

One of the biggest events in our city is the annual Calgary Stampede. When I was in my thirties, my buddies would kick off the ten-day event by going down to Cowboys, a dance hall and club, at 7:00 a.m. on Friday and start drinking and partying (it's a Calgary thing). And every kickoff Friday they'd call me, *all day long*, trying to get me to join them. But I was working. At that point I was general sales manager at Renfrew Chrysler.

It's not that I didn't enjoy partying with them, because I certainly did. I was simply driven to excel and knew what it took to do that. Though I missed out on some fun and many years of vacations back then, I'm now able to spend three months a year at my second home in Kelowna, British Columbia. I was willing to sacrifice an immediate reward to receive a greater reward later on. That's the essence of delayed gratification.

The point isn't to skip vacations and work yourself to death. The point is to understand that hard work pays off, and a willingness to sacrifice now can create tenfold enjoyment later. Having the passion we talked about earlier will make delayed gratification a whole lot easier.

Most people don't want to work that hard, which is good news if you like to. People take notice if you're the one making sacrifices. You'll be the one who comes to mind when promotions and opportunities come around. Remember John, the ambitious salesman? He was willing to sacrifice some sleep when others weren't, and he was rewarded with more car sales and more money in his paycheck. He also put himself in position for advancement when the time came.

My dad understood delayed gratification better than anyone. He followed his passion and worked right up until the end—grinding it out all along the way, knowing his hard work would pay off. And pay off it did. Dad passed at seventy-eight years old and never once had to worry about having enough money to pay bills. He was content and secure until the day he died because of how he cranked it in the decades prior. That grinding gene clearly runs in the family.

Grinders love to win. Like my dad, they are people of grit and perseverance who don't give up no matter what roadblocks they encounter. They just keep grinding.

The hardest part of grinding is the initial phase when you're still waiting for the payoff. It takes some true strength of character to step out and start cranking it when there are no guarantees that it will pay off. If I dangle the carrot of a bonus in front of my sales team, they will work hard in pursuit of that carrot. Still, there's no guarantee that their effort will get them the sales they need, but they certainly have a better chance than if they sat idle.

In the early eighties, Canada's economy was in the dumps. Interest rates were around 20 percent, and people were turning in their house keys to the banks. Dad was a young guy then and his company wasn't what it is now. He struggled at first, but he didn't give up. He made it through and the lessons he learned then carried him onward for the rest of his life.

Hardship is a refining fire; it's the difficult times where we learn our values and true selves. Dad ground past the pain and was better for it. Don't let hard times stop you from changing your life. The hardest times make you appreciate the things you weren't seeing.

NETWORKING

While working hard and creating your own luck, you can maximize your "luckiness" by being strategic in where you put your efforts. Networking is one of the best places to do this.

Whether or not you are selling something, you need to network. It takes time and effort to "shake hands and kiss babies," but the payoff is amazing. Because of my networking, I typically get five business or investment opportunities a month from people I've connected with. The more people you know, the more opportunities come up and the more luck you have.

You never know how meeting and connecting with someone now will help you down the road. Opportunities come to me in the oddest ways because of my network. I got to invest in a movie in California because of a friend I made at an event and made a whopping 50 percent return. You'll be surprised who offers you a job or other opportunity.

Besides new job opportunities, networking can build your credibility and give you the chance to find stronger players for your team. It also provides chances to learn from people in other industries, which can lead to new marketing ideas and more. You might even find a new career path, something you're really passionate about.

RISK-TAKING

Another place to make strategic effort is in the area of taking risks. You can go to school, work hard, network, and *really* crank it, but none of that will matter if you don't take the risk when the opportunity finally comes around.

Cleary, I mean *calculated* risk—don't run out to the casino after reading this chapter. Judge your opportunities accurately and choose what to "roll the dice" on. In 1972, my father did just that. I was a year-old baby and my dad had a great job working for Union Oil, making four grand a month—an incredible amount back then. My mother blew a gasket when he came home and told her he was leaving to buy a company. But he knew what he wanted, did his due diligence, and jumped on an incredible opportunity that paid off in big ways.

I love risk. People ask me how I can sleep at night and I always say, "On a big soft pillow." But I've been doing this a long time; I've grown comfortable with larger and larger risks. I'm also in a position to absorb those levels of loss, but I got there by taking smaller risks. Start where you are, with the level of risk you can manage. Not everybody is ready to start a new career right now.

My hard work and dedication to building relationships and an honest reputation has paid astounding dividends over the years. But it never would have happened if I hadn't acted on opportunities when they came up. Each time, I still had to take the risk.

A perfect example happened in 2006, when I was general sales manager at a Chrysler dealership in Edmonton. Because I had made sure there was no bad blood with Renfrew Chrysler when

I left two years earlier, the owner—the hardworking Mike Tarp I mentioned earlier—called me with an offer to come back.

"Mike, I'm happy in Edmonton," I said.

"Well, next time you're back in Calgary…"

The next time I was in Calgary was for the Stampede. I let Mike know I'd be there and we met at a sports lounge called Shanks. To my surprise, Dave Hoeght was there as well. Dave was the general manager when I was at Renfrew from 2002 to 2003, and then he had moved on. During my time at the dealership, Dave had returned to Renfrew in the same role.

"Come on, Dave. We want you back," Mike said coolly. But I stood my ground.

"Look, Mikey. I love hanging out with you; we're friends. But, I'm happy in Edmonton. It's like family up there—it's nice. I get two Sundays off a month and I'm making great money."

Mike took a long drink from his beer.

"Well, I actually want to sell you the store," Mike said.

That got my attention.

Mike continued, "Look, Dave is now CFO. I'd like to make you the general manager, make a bunch of money the next two years, and then you take 100 percent of the shares. And you can pay me for the store over time. Interested?"

My mind exploded with visions of the future. I saw the potential. This is exactly what I had been looking to do since I had left corporate.

On a bar napkin—where the best deals are made—we set up a contract where I would make the store $6 million over the next two years and then become the principal owner afterward. I'd then make payments to him at 5 percent interest for the store for the next five and a half years, a vendor take back (VTB). We agreed on a price of thirteen times the store's net profits—a high price, I know. But I love risks and this one had promise. The guy who looks like an idiot today, paying too much for real estate, for example, looks pretty smart ten years from now.

My relationship with Mike was what made this deal work so well. Most business owners want a big check when they sell their company. But because I had proven that I worked hard and brought results, Mike was willing to take the VTB route. And my luck got even better: Typically in a VTB, the owner will release more shares of the company while the principal is paid down. But on September 1, 2008, when I took over, Mike looked at me and said, "Dave, I don't want to deal with lawyers every year. I know you're good for it," and handed me 100 percent of the company.

On day one I owned my own dealership. How's that for creating your own luck.

MAXIMIZE YOUR LIFE

Your life is in your hands. You have the power to start making choices today and change your situation—you are the captain of your soul. Be honest enough to say what you really want and brave enough to chase after it. Not everyone is willing to do that; it's not easy. But you can make the choice. You can choose to start maximizing your life right now. Take the initiative to work hard, delay gratification, and open doors for yourself.

Just as hard work creates luck, being the most organized person in the room can make up for what you may lack in age or experience.

CHAPTER 4

PLANNING PRECEDES PERFORMANCE

After my bar napkin agreement with Mike Tarp in 2006, I set myself to developing the business plan of all business plans. I laid out everything from marketing to clientele to sales figures and revenue to who I would hire, what I would talk about at meetings, and everything in between.

At the time, Mike was enjoying semiretirement and was more of an absentee owner, spending most of his days on a beach in Florida. He called me after I faxed him the ten-page document.

"Dave, I've never seen something like this before."

"You like it?"

"Like it? I love it! This is the real deal! How did you come up with all this?"

"You know me, Mike. I never know when to quit."

Mike laughed. "Wow, this is great. You really think you can bump sales by 20 percent?"

"Absolutely. And if I don't, you can fire me."

"Not likely," Mike said, laughing again. "I'm pumped, Dave. I can't wait to get back. Let's do this."

How was I able to write something so impressive? It's not that I was a business plan-writing guru; it was my devotion to organization.

You don't have to be the smartest person on the team or in the boardroom, but if you're the most organized, you will be the smartest. People want to listen when you're organized. Planning and organization make you marketable and valuable at every stage of your career.

In this chapter, we'll look at the tips and tricks I've learned on organizing yourself and your team.

PERSONAL ORGANIZATION FIRST

Many people want a day's notice before receiving guests into their home. They want time to clean up and present themselves well. I never worry about people stopping by my home unannounced. Why? Because I keep my personal life as organized as my business life. You can come to my house at any time and it'll be in *mint* condition. My philosophy is, "If you can't manage your personal life, you can't manage a business."

When I hire a manager I pull their credit report. I want to see how well they handle their own affairs before they start managing mine.

If I can, I take a glance at their personal property as well, looking for signs of being well-groomed and well-organized. These types of things tell me that a person can handle their business.

Now, you don't need to be like me; I admit, I am a touch OCD. But, the truth remains that to be successful you do need to plan ahead. You need a certain level of organization. By making planning and organization habits in your personal life, they will naturally spill over into your professional life as well.

CREATE A SYSTEM

There are lots of systems, programs, and ways to help you set goals and organize your life. I'm old-school; I've been using my pen-and-paper binder system for the past two decades. Other people use their phones. Find something that works for you and use it.

I carry around a notepad like a Bible—my employees affectionately call it "The Pad." When something comes up that I need to do, I write it down and date it. Typically these are daily tasks ranging from returning phone calls to helping my managers with their projects. When I complete the task, I check it off. If I don't get to something that day, I transfer it to the next day's page, and so on, and so on, until it's done. Completed pages go into a yearly binder.

While I use The Pad for keeping track of tactical day-to-day tasks, I use a whiteboard for long-term strategic planning for the business. If we're looking at buying a new dealership, for example, and we want to revisit the decision in three months, that goes on the whiteboard. So do other future plans like courses to hone skills and real estate expansion projects. The short-term tasks related to those long-term plans go on The Pad.

DEVELOP A ROUTINE

Routines are healthy in life and business; they create predictability and accountability, both for yourself and others. If you have a daily routine of showing up to work on time, you'll hesitate before going out and drinking until five in the morning. Routines are also a declaration that you will not have a "throwaway day," that you have a plan and you're sticking to it.

Every morning I wake up early and stop by the grocery store. I say hello to the employees there, buy strawberries and an orange, and eat those for breakfast while I check my emails. I wanted to eat well and take care of emails early in the day, so I built a habit around both.

Another daily routine involves looking at my attitude checklist before I ever leave the house.

KEEP A DAILY ATTITUDE CHECKLIST

My attitude checklist is the list of traits that I am working on to improve my life. By reading this list first thing in the morning, I am oriented in the right direction from the second I wake up to the moment I hit the pillow, ensuring that I never have a throwaway day.

My attitude checklist is the plan for my plan: I can't accomplish my personal or business goals without getting my head right first.

Here's my list and my reasons behind each item, but you should figure out how you want to show up every day, make a list, and start keeping yourself accountable.

Nail the First Impression

When I first started my career, I wore my finest suit and polished my shoes to a mirror shine every day. These days, I'm a bit more casual, but I still shave every morning and get a haircut every week. As we all know, first impressions only happen once, and I remind myself every day that I need to nail it when I meet someone new.

You only have about two minutes at most when making a first impression. If you start a relationship off on the wrong foot, it's extremely difficult to get back to someone's good graces. How you present yourself is a reflection of how you *feel* about yourself: your pride (the good kind). Even if they don't say anything, people notice this.

So, set yourself up for success by wearing your best clothes and smiling when you meet people. You never know when you'll meet the person who causes your career to take off—remember what I said about creating your own luck? Come in every day fresh and ready to roll.

Stay Positive

I continually remind myself to keep a positive attitude. If I have a bad day, I'll think about it for five minutes the next morning and then forget about it. I thank God for what I have *this* day, such as still being alive and healthy. Why would I take a nosedive into self-loathing and spend the next twenty years having a pity party going over all the things that have gone wrong? No thanks.

If you let yesterday affect today, you just wind up with another bad day, and the same will happen tomorrow, the next day, and so on, causing you to miss out on so many potential opportunities.

Take five minutes to think about what went wrong, change what you can, and get on with it.

Don't Be Jealous

Every day I remind myself to cast off jealousy. It does nothing but dampen my spirits and cause rifts in my relationships.

"The enemy is not your fellow salesperson; it's the other dealerships" is one of my favorite sayings in the car business, but it applies to *all* businesses. The team you are on is exactly that—a *team*: a group of people all working together to achieve a common goal, helping each other accomplish more than any single team member could alone. People tend to forget this, or just don't understand how helping others is actually helping themselves. When I help out and train a general manager to become a better leader, it comes back around to me—typically, as more sales.

You and your team are all in this together; *it's not a competition.* There's no room for jealousy in a team. If one guy sells twenty cars and the others each sell fifteen, they should all be happy for the team. When my brother Doug has an amazing year with his commercial refrigeration company, I'm happier than he is; plus, it motivates me to go even further in my business. No green-eyed monster in these parts.

Be Respectful

Being respectful came up when we discussed being a team player, and it's something I focus on every day. When I come into the dealership each morning, my goal is to respect everyone I talk to. I also respect my family and friends by going to dinner with them when they extend an invitation. When people feel respected they respond in turn; they, like you, understand giving and receiving respect.

Hang Out with the Right People

You've probably heard the theory that we are the sum of the five people we hang out with. I have found this to be true. I am where I am today because of the company I've held, both professionally and personally. I keep a close circle of friends who do the right thing, are positive influences, and exude good karma. I spend my time with people who are better than me so I can "bring up my average." If I golf with people who shoot ninety-five, I will have about the same number of strokes, but if I play with a scratch golfer my game plummets by eight to ten strokes.

Time is the most precious resource on the planet; we are all allotted a certain amount in this life. Every day, I make sure I'm spending it with quality people who positively affect my life.

Don't Give Up

As I've said, I'm a grinder, like my dad. But I still have to remind myself daily not to give up.

When I first submitted my application to purchase Renfrew Chrysler in 2008, two years after my napkin deal with Mike Tarp, I was not given an immediate yes or no answer. Instead, my application sat in someone's in-basket for months. This could have been a major roadblock to my goals and could have left me dead in my tracks, but I knew better than to give up—I was a fighter. There was no way of getting around the regional manager who was blocking me from my goal because of my young age, so I set myself to do what I had always done: work hard, be honest, and do right. I kept my nose to the grindstone, sold more cars, and kept improving our service.

Life is tough. Every day things will happen that cause you to want to give up on your goals. I've had plenty of good reasons to give up during my journey, but I didn't and now look where I am. Certainly, there are times to call it quits, but if your goals are feasible and realistic and you are simply experiencing some challenges, keep going.

Listen, Listen, and Listen Again

It's easy to do all the talking, especially when you're in management, but there's a reason we have two ears and one mouth, right? If we're listening, we're learning—and if we're talking, *we aren't listening*. We all have things to learn every day, so we have to remind ourselves to ask questions and then listen to the answer.

Listening is also a way to show people you care. When I was courting my girlfriend, I listened a whole bunch. By keeping my mouth shut, I noticed how excited she was when talking about the NFL. So, naturally, this hockey lover became a football fan in record time. Is that "cheating the system"? Nope. It's showing other people that you care about what is important to them.

Have Fun

On a lighter note, it's important to relax a little. Think about the guy in your workplace who's fun-loving; you just want to be around him. This even works in dating. Take the guy who's a seven out of ten in looks but give him a good sense of humor and suddenly he's a nine out of ten overall.

This characteristic comes more naturally to some people, but it's nothing that can't be developed. People like to work with, be around, and buy things from people they like. It's a worthwhile attitude to develop.

The day-to-day workload can get stressful, and strategic planning can be exhausting. We all need time to have fun and recharge. To take my mind off work, I spend time at my home in Kelowna, relaxing and boating with friends. We cruise the lake with the music playing and stop at a few restaurants along the shoreline. We don't discuss business, yet these free days tend to open my mind to creative solutions.

Boating may not be your thing, but find a way to unwind and enjoy time laughing and creating memories with family and friends. Chances are you'll bring that same fun, relaxed spirit into the workplace, making you an enjoyable person to have on any team.

Execute

Each morning, I hit my knees and pray so I can be focused and make the most out of my day. My singular motivation is to work toward my goals. The notepad I carry around is worthless if I don't execute the tasks I write down.

Execution is the follow-through, like finishing a check in hockey. When there is a deadline, meet it. When you say you will handle something, do it—and no excuses if you don't. When you decide to jump on a new opportunity, don't put off the follow-through or you might miss the window.

You don't have to be as intense as me—I'm just bred that way—but you do need to understand that your goals will never come about without some follow-through. As Antoine de Saint-Exupéry once said, "A goal without a plan is just a wish."

Leave Your Problems Where They Belong

No matter what is going on in my personal life, I walk into Renfrew every day with a big smile. When people ask me how I'm doing I always answer, "Never better!" They don't need to know what's happening outside the dealership. Do you want to know if the sales representative at a shoe store recently broke up with her partner? Probably not. You just want her help buying a pair of shoes.

Likewise, I don't take my work problems home. I leave my problems wherever they belong so I can be "on" no matter where I am.

No Shortcuts

There are no shortcuts in life. No one wakes up and finds success without grinding and making sacrifices—I certainly didn't. What I did in my twenties and thirties has paid major dividends in my fifties. I crank it every day in my fifties to have the same happen in my sixties.

To make sure I don't skip steps, I consult The Pad as soon as I get to work each day. I make sure I handle the priorities and carry over the other tasks, but I don't skip them entirely or take a shortcut to get something done quicker.

Every day there will be opportunities to cut corners. Don't do it. Shortcuts can cost you money, success, or even a promotion you were hoping for. The payoff for doing it right is worth it.

No Throwaway Days

Throwaway days are days that don't count because you aren't giving your best. Every morning I remind myself that I have an opportunity to grow, to better myself, to push toward my goals. It takes discipline to wake up every morning at 5:00 a.m. and roll up my sleeves, but the payoff is knowing I did my best. And should something go wrong, I'll never wonder what else I could have done.

Every single second of every single day should be used productively. Develop your routine, deliver your daily pep talk, and make the most of the opportunities you are given.

TEAM ORGANIZATION

Organization is important in every business, every organization, every team. It puts people at ease because they see the plan. They know what is expected.

That said, being organized is a bit more important on the corporate side. If you walk into a corporate meeting unprepared and disorganized, you'll be ridiculed for wasting everyone's time. Retailers, on the other hand, can often make due with their personality and salesmanship. If you know you aren't all that organized and want to get into a corporate position, take time to learn this skill first. It will carry you a long way.

No matter where you land, a key part of planning and organization in the business world involves goal setting on multiple levels—yearly, monthly, weekly, daily—and then setting up accountability checkpoints to make sure you're on track.

ACCOUNTABILITY CHECKPOINTS

Every December I ask myself the same question: "What do I want to achieve next year?" Identifying longer-term goals and writing them down accomplishes a few things. One, it helps you see what you want and create a plan to get there—you can't hit a target you can't see. Two, it keeps you accountable—you can't wiggle your way out of a goal you explicitly wrote down.

In sports, a coach might tell a hockey center he wants fifty goals this season and then follow up with, "How are you going to make that happen?" The center might respond with, "Well, coach, I'm going to come to every practice an hour early and work on my shot." In life and in business, you need to be your own coach. You set the goals for yourself and your team and then ask yourself, "How are we going to make this happen?" Then write down your answers.

I know that this will be the best year Renfrew Chrysler has ever had because I planned it that way. Steve MacDonald and I are being proactive in doing what we think will work best. If April comes around and our numbers are low, we will simply readjust. I don't chase life. I set mine up to perform the way I want it to.

Yearly goals are great "big picture" items, but you can't stop there;

you need checkpoints throughout the year to keep you on track. As I always say, it's easy to look through a microscope but difficult to be under it. When under the microscope, you're exposed and accountable. When you look through it, you can zoom in, which is exactly what you need to do with your goals. Break up your yearly goals into analyzable chunks so you can check your progress more regularly, say, every quarter.

For example, if I decided to sell 3,000 cars this year, I know that by the end of March I need to have sold around 750. If I haven't, I readjust and make a plan to catch up and have 1,500 sold by the end of the second quarter. Doing this keeps me from chasing the market—I won't be shaking at the knees, wondering, "What to do?! What to do?!" if I come up short. Everything is already laid out.

The same checkpoint principle is used in the smaller goals. Each quarter can be broken down into its months, each month into its weeks, and weeks into days. Using the same arithmetic as above, I know that in the third week of June I need to sell around sixty cars—about ten cars a day. Having all this information laid out allows you to see where you are at any given moment.

This is just simple division based upon a larger goal—you don't need to be a rocket scientist to succeed here.

ROUTINES

Just as routines will help you stay on track personally, they'll also help your team. Daily routines and planning give people the solidity they are looking for, and as their leader, you need to give it to them. Nobody likes to have a meeting for the sake of having a meeting, but if you can lay down an organized plan, for the year down to the day, you'll get a positive reaction from your team.

I meet with my crew every morning, at the same time per our daily routine. We go over where they are in sales, what they need to do that day, and what is needed to accomplish that day's or week's goal. For a time, I also held daily one-on-one meetings with each team member to build up personal relationships and create camaraderie. Both types of meetings worked like a charm. People knew the routine and responded to it: they were pumped to meet their own goals.

NO ROCK UNTURNED

Whether you are corporate or retail, early in your career or the new CEO, the truth remains: planning precedes performance. At this point in my career, I've purchased a number of dealerships. I'm familiar with the process. Yet every time I approach a bank for a loan, I spend hours ahead of time preparing for my meeting with the senior bank vice president. And every time, I secure the loan in the amount I've asked for. Would I get the loan if walked into the meeting cold, with no thought about how to present my request? Probably not, or at least not for the amount I'm seeking.

You may not be at the level of acquiring businesses, but the same mindset applies to preparing for a job interview. Don't walk into the interview cold turkey. Take time to learn about the company: the backstory (Is it family owned? How many generations?), the values they have posted on the website, and so on. Also find out the little details: where you need to park, how long it will take to get there, which route is less likely to have delays.

Organizational skills will serve you no matter which business path you take, corporate or retail. That's just one of the skills you need to hone as you advance your career. We'll discuss several others next.

CHAPTER 5

IMPROVING SKILLS THROUGH TRAINING

When I took the general sales manager job at Renfrew in 2002, I had to leave my work family in Maple Ridge, which was very hard. We often shared dinners together and visited each other's homes, and I had really connected with the community.

But my leaving turned into one of the best compliments I've ever received. In the world of sales, especially at a car dealership, when you quit, you walk out that day. It's not personal; it's just a sales thing. When I told Maple Ridge I was leaving, however, they kept me on for two and a half weeks.

This spoke volumes about the relationships I had made there and the trust I had built. They knew I was the type of man to not try and steal their customers. It was emotional to be sure, but they understood what an amazing offer I had, and they gave me the warmest send-off possible.

Whether you're in corporate or retail, relationships are a big part of your job. If you understand the chain of command, respect others, and show people you genuinely care, you will reap the benefits. In this chapter we'll consider other important skills that will improve your chances of success and make you a better person.

CORPORATE VS. RETAIL

The biggest difference between corporate and retail is that with a corporate job you have a salary while retail is all commission-based—expecting X amount of pay every two weeks versus "eating what you kill."

Choosing your path often comes down to personality. Some people are drawn to the security and polish of corporate jobs where they have a clear ladder to climb. Others have an itch and nothing will scratch it except getting out there and rolling the dice in retail; they thrive on the risk and reward. I have seen talented and aggressive corporate employees excel in that realm and then fail miserably when they try their hand at retail.

Another deciding factor is your interests and passion. If you have a passion for clothing, for example, and feel you'd make a good buyer, seek out a position at a fashion company's head office. Spend a few years learning the corporate side of the clothing industry—while getting paid—and later decide if you want to retire with the company or step out and open a store. On the other hand, if you have passion along with a healthy love of risk, you might go the retail route—more power to you; you're my type of person. Be sure to develop some thick skin and take some notes from this book when you do.

Bottom line: there's no right or wrong route. Every person is different. As long as you are building skills and taking action, you really can't go wrong.

CORPORATE

The qualities and attitudes we've discussed so far apply whether you go corporate or retail. Passion, listening skills, hard work, persistence—these will get you on the team in any industry. There are a few qualities that are more important in corporate over retail and vice versa. We'll start with corporate.

Know How to Write

As mentioned earlier, being well-written is *vital* in corporate. This skill earns you respect with your fellow employees and, more importantly, with the person to whom you are writing. It can give you an edge when promotion time comes around, and it can add credibility to your resume.

Likewise, a lack of writing skills can reflect on you negatively. A dealer I know received a letter from the head office that expressed concerns about the performance of the dealership. Because the letter was so poorly written, the dealer didn't take the concerns seriously and threw it out.

We salesmen can often get away with a lot, but the corporate environment has funny idiosyncrasies—"how well you write" being one of them. If you draft a well-written letter and copy the regional manager, you may be seen as "educated" or "intelligent" in someone's mind, and that someone may remember your skill when it comes time for a promotion.

Whenever I received a corporate letter that impressed me, I'd put it in a binder to save as a reference. Down the line when I had to write someone, I would flip through my binder and find an old letter that matched what I wanted to convey. I'd then model my message by copying the flow, word choice, and grammar, and send off the letter, CC'ing my boss. It was a simple process but it made me look like a genius.

WRITING A BUSINESS PLAN

As you read in Chapter 4, I wrote the business plan of all business plans when I had the opportunity to buy Renfrew Chrysler. My thoroughness and attention to detail are part of what impressed Mike Tarp, as well as my ability to present my ideas clearly. Here again, writing skills come into play.

Here are some basic tips for writing your own business plan. For a more detailed explanation, see *The Secrets to Writing a Successful Business Plan* by Hal Shelton.

- First and foremost, don't *over*write the plan using big words and many paragraphs. Write in clear, simple language, direct and to the point—all meat and potatoes. The reader wants a quick snapshot of the overall objective.
- Start with a brief discussion of your background and your accomplishments:
  - Education
  - Work history
  - Some success stories you have accomplished (just a few; no need to overdo it)
  - Awards and accolades (but don't brag)
- Speak about your current team, or the team you want to establish:
  - Who will make up your team
  - Why they should be on the team
  - The potential team members' education, track record, reputation, résumé with accomplishments, envisioned future accomplishments

- Describe your company, or the company you want to invest in:
  - Organizational chart
  - Brief synopsis of the company or startup business: How many staff, market conditions, sales, profitability, marketing, cash flow, financing in place, future growth plans, sales projection years one to five
  - Include résumés for everyone on the team/company
- Products and services the company provides or will provide:
  - Why you believe in it
  - Why it will work
  - Competition in the field
  - Current sales/net profit
- Marketing
  - What is being done now in terms of digital marketing, social media, and mining the database you currently have
  - What you will do in the future to market the company
  - Percentage of marketing dollars to sales
- Identify who you want to attract as future employees:
  - Characteristics: strong work ethic, honest, solid reputation
  - Education: level of education or field of study
  - Experience: previous successes and accolades, number of years in the field
- Discuss whether you are looking for funding from a bank or personal investments:
  - How much you need and why
  - How long to pay it back (loan term)
  - Return on the investment
- Describe the financial projections of the company:
  - Be conservative
  - Justify the projections

In addition, perform a SWOT analysis to help you identify the **S**trengths, **W**eaknesses, **O**pportunities, and **T**hreats involved in the proposed business proposition. Include this SWOT analysis as part of your plan.

Here are some examples of what you might identify in each category:

- Strengths:

- Large customer base
- Advanced technology
- Strong investors
- Team with the skills and knowledge to take on the opportunity
- Bank financing is in place, creating chance for strong cash flow
- Weaknesses:
  - Lack of supply and/or substandard supply chain
  - New brand that hasn't been tested in the market
  - Heavy debt load with long-term loan for paying it back
  - Lack of proven investors
  - High staff turnover in the industry
  - Business location
  - Lack of customer database
- Opportunities:
  - Having a competitive edge
  - Chance to apply your strengths
  - Competition's customers are unhappy
  - New supply chains
  - Lack of marketing in the industry
  - Lack of stock in the industry
- Threats:
  - Areas of potential loss for your business
  - Increased salaries in the industry
  - Unorganized supply chain that cannot keep up with demands
  - Poor cash flow
  - Excessive employee turnover
  - New competition coming

Finally, make sure your business plan has a strong conclusion based on the SWOT analysis and the rest of the points made. Sum up what you hope to accomplish, how your company will successfully hit the target market, and how you're ready to hit the ground running. A well-structured business plan will help you set and meet your short- and long-term goals.

Know How to Adapt to Situations and People

If tomorrow morning I was invited to the White House for breakfast and later that evening to a motorcycle rally, I'd fit in with both crowds. Adapting like this has everything to do with emotional intelligence—being able to read the room, understand the vibe, know what is appropriate and not. Really, it's simply being aware of those around you and making adjustments accordingly.

Adaptability paired with solid communication skills is one of the most effective traits you can develop. Some people are certainly more naturally gifted in these areas but both communication skills and adaptability can be learned.

RETAIL

When I made the switch to retail, it was an eye-opener, to say the least. No one handed me an instruction manual. I had to learn by osmosis and watch how other people worked, and sometimes it felt like I had been thrown to the wolves to learn on my own.

But I loved it. When I went home each night I had trouble falling asleep because my adrenaline was still pumping from the intense energy and rapid-paced environment. I thrived on the challenge of being compensated based on my production. I controlled my earnings, not some salary cap.

It takes a certain kind of person to make it in retail, but from my observations and experience, the following seven skills can make you a successful salesperson.

Understand the Chain of Command

You definitely need this skill in corporate as well, but I want to highlight how it's important in retail. As a district manager, you don't skip over the regional sales manager to talk to the regional manager—that's a good way to paint a target on your back. Follow the chain of command. Passing over someone is effectively saying, "What you did to earn this position is not important." If you want to step on someone's toes, there are few better ways to go about it, in corporate or retail.

At my dealership, I don't let anyone complain to me about their boss. I tell them to talk to that person, and if they don't like that answer, they can find another place of employment.

Be Sold on Yourself

You can't help anyone if you don't believe in yourself first, and you certainly won't win the sale if you come across as unconfident. Whether people come into a dealership or a shoe store, they want to work with someone who shows confidence in themself and their product.

This is true in all occupations. Take a doctor, for example. To save someone's life, he needs to be confident in his medical ability. If a doctor comes in and I sense that he's not sure of what he's doing, I ask for another doctor.

Someone who is sold on herself exudes confidence in her posture: shoulders back, head up, brisk and purposeful walk. Confident people *know* what they can do. They can ask the questions that challenge, intrigue, and impress—they make the light bulb turn on, so to speak. These signs give *me* the confidence to believe in *their* confidence. They aren't cocky, however. Cockiness creates a different challenge that sends people running in the other direction.

Why do people visit the same bar four nights a week? Because they like the bartender. The drinks and the price are the same everywhere, but Bar X is the only one where Bobby is serving drinks, and Bobby knows what he's doing. He's confident without being cocky.

I'm sold on the fact I'm a good person and want to help people, and I know that today I'll be selling myself. When I ask someone to dinner, I'm selling that it will be a fun time—that I'll be entertaining and share great stories. At work, my confidence communicates that I'm somebody who gets things done. Naturally, people catch on to that and instinctively trust me, letting me make the sale.

Develop and Maintain a Sales Plan

Remember our discussion of planning and organization? That comes into play here.

Sales plans are simple and everyone's plan is basically the same, from the boss to those working the sales floor. Say that you're selling vacuums and want to make twenty sales a month. You know from experience (or from your boss) that vacuum sales have about a 10 percent closing ratio. With some simple mathematics, you know that you need to talk to two hundred people to make twenty sales. You also know that the marketing flyers you send out have a 5 percent response rate and with the same arithmetic you calculate you need to send out four thousand flyers to get two hundred leads. With that in mind, you're also aware that your $1,000 cleaning machine is only affordable for white-collar, affluent people, so you target those areas with your marketing.

Being in sales is simple, actually. It's basic math with some personal skills. Break down your process to develop your plan, observe its effectiveness, and adjust from there, learning as you go.

Become an Effective Communicator

Salespeople must be incredible communicators. Their entire job can be boiled down to telling a customer how they need a product or service. Two of the best communication practices you can develop are reading people and speaking with them in their preferred style, whether that's text, phone, email, or video chat. My brother loves to chat over speakerphone so my sister-in-law is included in the conversation, and it's a great way to stay connected. As much as I dislike using FaceTime, I do it with others to earn their friendship, and I would do it with a high-powered executive in the corporate office if that's how he wanted to check in with me.

It's your responsibility to communicate your message clearly, simply, and in a way that's readily understood. How can you tell if your message is hitting the mark? Check out your recipients' responses. They are the best indicator of whether they understand your message.

Use Time Wisely

I can do in four hours what most men can do in ten because I make every second count. I come in with my mind ready, my routine set, and my day organized. In short, I'm ready to go full throttle from the moment I step into the building.

When I used to smoke, I'd watch others on their smoke break. Some guys would be out there for an hour. *Why were they even at work?* To a point, the number of hours you work is irrelevant; if all your "effort" is unproductive, there's no difference between coming to work and taking the day off.

Spend time on things that matter, things that will really make a difference. Focusing on the nonnegotiables will make your life more manageable, more productive, and less stressful.

See Technology as a Tool, Not a Crutch

Most adults my age are scared to learn new things, especially when it comes to technology. This was my exact response when Microsoft Excel came around. I kept hearing how great the software was, but I didn't want to take the time to figure it out. Then I finally sat down one day and made myself learn it. By the time I finished, I'd had a complete paradigm shift. Excel was revolutionary for organizing my business; I still have some of the spreadsheets I made years ago. Once I'd seen how this tool helped me crank it even more, I wanted all I could get my hands on.

That said, technology can be a crutch, something you lean on too heavily instead of doing the work yourself. This often happens when technology replaces human connection. For example, there are easy ways to automatically have birthday cards sent out to your customers—you can even upload a digital signature so you never have to look at or read the card you're sending. But people know when a card is from some automatic system.

Better to put in the extra effort to handwrite notes and let people know you care.

Genuinely Care about Others

Hopefully, this one speaks for itself: if you genuinely care for others and seek what's best for them, people take notice and remember.

When people walk into a retail store of any kind, everyone knows why they're there: to make a purchase. The buyer is going to spend money, and the salesperson is going to make money on a sale. That said, if a dishonest salesman smooth-talks you into a bad deal, you'll never go back to his car lot, and you might tell all your friends not to either. But if you go to a dealership and a salesperson listens to your concerns, gives you time to decide, answers questions without sounding annoyed, and makes sincere suggestions based on what you shared, you'll walk away with a positive experience—and you'll be more likely to return as a result.

People know the difference between focusing on the sale and focusing on people to get the sale.

Currently, I'm looking to invest in some real estate. My Realtor and I found some properties and I was ready to pull the trigger. However, my Realtor advised me against it and said we should wait to find a better deal. He saw some things that weren't quite right with the investment, and while he could have made a quick buck, he counseled me to wait. I appreciate his honesty, and I'm more likely to use him as my Realtor down the road.

Moral of the story: care about others and you'll be a better salesperson.

PICK YOUR PATH

Now that you've considered some aspects of corporate and retail, which direction will you go? As I've said, there's no right or wrong answer; it's just a matter of knowing yourself and what you want:

- Are you a risk-taker?
- Do you like the security of a steady paycheck?
- Would you make sacrifices to work extra hours and to make an extra sale?
- Do you like having a clear path up the ladder of advancement?

If you have the opportunity to try both retail and corporate experience, go for it. As you've seen, many of the skills apply in both. Plus, if you can test the waters in each, then you'll really know which path is for you.

Whether you choose corporate or retail, at some point you will move beyond being a player to building your own team.

CHAPTER 6

BUILD YOUR TEAM

When I came to Renfrew Chrysler in 2006, I knew it was important to start with a core group of experienced managers. Renfrew had a fairly solid management team in place, but I wanted to add some new people to stir the pot and introduce some large changes.

I started with a blank sheet of paper and created three lists: who to keep, who to promote (or demote), and who to let go. Once that was laid out, I started brainstorming people to add to the team. Next to each name, I added a note on why they should be added so I could justify my decisions with the remaining managers.

After the moves were made, the dealership experienced about a month of dysfunction because the managers who stayed on had a hard time adjusting to the changes. It was a tough month, no doubt, but it ultimately paid off. I had a handpicked team that led Renfrew to great success.

After being on a team and cranking it for a good while, no doubt that you'll be the one who starts putting teams together. While similar in many ways, retail and corporate teams have a few distinct differences. Let's take a look.

BUILDING A TEAM

Remember that list from Chapter 1, qualities to build in yourself if you want to make the team? The same applies here. Look for those who are passionate, disciplined, polite, generous, and positive—all-around good people who listen and help others. Here are a few other considerations when you're the one putting the team together, whether you've landed on the retail or corporate side.

BRING ON PEOPLE YOU TRUST

Trust is such an important aspect of building an effective, productive team. I have learned the hard way at times that some people say, "Trust me; I have your back," when in truth they only care about themselves. I could write a chapter on this topic alone.

Building your team around people you trust is vital to your success. Pick people you know are in it for the long haul, people who have shown their trustworthiness over time.

A prime example is Steve MacDonald, my CFO. We had been friends for thirty-five years when I hired him, so I knew he would be a valuable asset to the team. I knew he wouldn't steal ten cents if he could. Having someone like Steve to depend on is priceless in business. Plus, because of our closeness, Steve is comfortable calling me out when I'm wrong—which I desperately need. If I'm making a bad decision, he'll put me back in line because he has my best interests at heart.

Finding someone like Steve can be tough, but it is possible. Always be on the lookout for people who share your values and would jump right in to support the vision you're creating. A past history together is a bonus but not a must.

FIND PEOPLE WHO FIT

When you find potential candidates for your team, you'll need to vet them before bringing them on. Check their track record and reputation. The spots on a leopard don't change; better to know what kind of team members you're getting beforehand so you can decide if they fit your criteria.

If I know the person being used as a reference, I'll call to get more information because I'll know they're being straight with me; their answers will not be fabricated. I'll also call references I don't know, but I'm aware they might simply tell me what I want to hear.

Information that's helpful for understanding a person's track record:

- How long have they been at each job?
- If they've been at one or more jobs for a short time (say, less than six months), find out why
- What accolades did they receive at past jobs?
- Who is in their inner circle of friends?

Length of time at past jobs is especially important in terms of dependability and building a team. You want to know someone waters their own lawn rather than looking for greener pastures.

Equally important, however, is going with your gut. If a candidate left a job after four months, I would ask why. If I found out it's because she didn't click with her manager, and everything else about this person really checks out, I would probably conclude that her last manager was the problem and offer her the job.

Ideally, you can create a team with people you've known for many years and already have a true sense of their character and whether they share your work ethic and values. When I hired Steve, I'd known him for more than three decades, so I knew his reputation well. I also knew we'd take a bullet for each other.

A quick note on hiring friends: I took a risk hiring Steve because business partnerships ruin friendships on the regular. But, if they work out, nothing is better than working with someone you know, love, and trust. I felt confident with Steve and was candid when I made him the offer. Thirteen years later we are still going strong, even expanding operations; it's been a true blessing.

At the same time, I've had many friends come to me wanting to get into the car business, and I often tell them no. They aren't bad people; they're just not the right fit. We don't click—mostly because they're only after the money. When Steve and I first spoke about working together, I knew he wasn't chasing the dollar: his first question was "What can I bring to this team?" not "How much will I make this year?" He wanted a career where he could contribute and be part of a winning team. He wanted to enhance the business by bringing in skills and experience we didn't have in place. Based on our conversation, I could tell he'd be great with finances. Dave Hoeght, the CFO at the time, was soon retiring, so I had Steve train under Dave and take his place after he retired.

Beyond seeing how his skills could help me and the team, I knew

Steve wouldn't cause me any brain damage. To this day Steve has never played the friend card and has always been early with his reports. If you feel that your friend would work well with you, it may be worth the risk. Just don't go in blind.

COMPLEMENT, NOT COMPLICATE

You want to have people on your team who have complementary skillsets. I love marketing and public speaking, but I hate being the "bad guy." Steve, on the other hand, can deliver hard news like a pro. I am more of a risk-taker. I shoot and clean up later. Steve analyzes the situation and makes a more calculated decision. In one case, I was ready to pull the trigger and buy a Nissan dealership.

"Slow down, Dave," Steve said. "Let's look at how long the lease is. How soon till we can purchase the land and building?"

Come to find out it was only a one-year lease, and we needed two years to build the new building. I may have found the deal in the first place, but it was Steve who got the best deal. We complement each other and make a better team for it.

Finding complementing skillsets is an art form and almost has to come from getting to know a group's culture before its construction. But, while building a team, be sure to consider each person's role and how they will function with the other members' skills.

ALL WORK AND NO PLAY...

More than collecting a group of functional individuals for a specific purpose, building a team is about building comradery. I get to know my people and encourage them to do the same with each other. Every month I host a "kickoff meeting," which is more like a party where we catch up and then handle business.

You're not going to be able to do everything yourself. Build your team and take care of them—like family. Create a tight-knit group of people who all love each other and feel like they belong. Lead by example and start getting involved with their lives.

NOT MAKING THE CUT

Obviously, if your team is not meeting their goals, something is wrong—something is unhealthy. If so, start by looking inward. All business is management-driven, not market-driven, employee-driven, or luck-driven. Business always starts, and ends, at the top. Even back when Calgary's oil was at eighteen dollars a barrel, our dealership still had fantastic years because of the management.

If someone is pointing fingers related to their failing business, I always say they have more windows than mirrors in their house: they spend more time looking outward than inward. If you and/ or your team are struggling, start by looking at your day-to-day plans. Remember what I said about throwaway days? Many times it's the little things that add up and create large issues.

When I wasn't making the cut, I started coming in an hour earlier to meet with my sales team every single morning. I would get updates on where they were, check to see if they were following up with customers, and ask how I could help. I looked at the numbers, saw the deficiencies, made a plan, and stuck to it every day until the problem was solved.

Look at the issues you are having and adapt this proactive approach to your business. Create a daily process of actionable steps that you can follow and grind through every day.

CORPORATE TEAMS

When I was initially hired by Chrysler, I was fresh out of university and had zero experience. I got the job based on my education and competitiveness in sports. Yes, my hockey experience helped land me that first job. Businesses know that people who are competitive in sports are usually competitive in business too, always pushing to be better. Keep this in mind if the person does not have experience on paper.

In addition, you have the interview. People tend to tell you what you want to hear, so you need to read between the lines. I look for passion in how people talk about themselves, their accomplishments, and what they bring to the table. I also want to know if they've researched the company and can tell me why the job is a good fit.

RETAIL TEAMS

Though there are many similarities between corporate and retail teams, they do have some differences. For example, education is one of the biggest factors in corporate; in some cases, a four-year degree is a must. In retail, however, personality is often more important because it takes charisma and drive to secure sales and succeed.

As they say, better the devil you know than the devil you don't. This proverb has rung true all throughout my career. I *never* put out job postings and hope the right person will apply; it's a recipe for disaster in my experience. I always promote from within, and if I don't have the right person, or if that person isn't ready for that responsibility yet, I poach someone from another business or dealership.

For example, back in 2010 I found one of my best salespeople tending a bar. Ricky was personable, and he could sell a drink. So I offered him a job selling cars along with a nice signing bonus, and he snatched it up. Ricky worked hard and learned quickly, and he became a manager before moving on to another opportunity. I found another great salesman when I bought a phone at Best Buy. I gave him the same offer I gave Ricky, and now he's selling twenty-five cars a month.

Building a team like this takes some out-of-the-box thinking. In your day-to-day interactions, you should be aware of what qualities people possess and how you could help one another. The only thing you need after that is the guts to walk up to a prospect and be a little brash.

I have something of a spiel ready when I meet people I want to hire. I typically start with a compliment on their skills: I'll tell them how I'm impressed with their ability to hold a conversation with me when I'm twenty-five years their senior, or how they carry themselves with unarrogant confidence. Then I'll let them know why I'm approaching them and say something like, "Salesmanship is salesmanship no matter where you are, but you can make a lot of dough selling cars. Plus, you'll start a career versus just collecting a check."

Modify this strategy to fit your needs. Think about why someone should join you and sell your company to them. A big tip: people want to work at a place that's enjoyable. Be joyful and excited about your business when you're talking to prospects. Between offering someone a career, more coin, and a great place to work, you'll have very few rejections and build up a skilled team in no time.

But let it be made clear, I'm genuine when I do this; I don't make offers to every waitress or salesman I meet. If I truly believe someone would work well for me, I tell them; if I don't, I keep my mouth shut. Being honest is doubly effective because people can tell when you're just feeding them a line. When you are genuine, it shows, and people can't resist you.

YOU'RE ONLY AS GOOD AS YOUR TEAM

Write this down and remember it: you're only as good as your team. Therefore, it's important to surround yourself with people who are smarter and more skilled than you, especially in the areas where you aren't as strong. I know my qualities, what I excel at. I'm good at marketing and putting together business deals, but I'm not a detail guy, so I hire people who are. Then we work together to make sure every aspect of the business as a whole and each individual deal is covered.

A major part of building a strong team is being the kind of coach/ leader people will follow.

CHAPTER 7

BE A COACH PEOPLE WANT TO PLAY FOR

My dad, brother, and I loved cars. We were fanatics—any classic automobile from the 1960s had us drooling. My preteen years were filled with car shows, car magazines, and talks around the dinner table about whether or not the 1971 Hemi 'Cuda could beat a 1967 Corvette Tri-power—poor Mom had to start loving cars just to be involved in the conversations! But more than getting to revel in my love of cars, what made it all so special was sharing it with my family.

In 1995, I went to my first big auction with my dad and brother— the Barrett Jackson in Scottsdale, Arizona. It blew my mind. There must have been more than two thousand cars hitting the auction block with no reserve, meaning every car would sell to the highest bidder, no matter what that bid was or the current market value of the car. Some of these cars were worth more than a million dollars back then; they would break the bank today. We sat in the bidders lounge, watching each car go over the block and guessing how much each one would sell for. People around us were astonished at how much my brother and I knew about each car and how close we came to guessing the actual selling price.

As mentioned, my mom took advantage of this passion and used it to help with my education. I read about every type of car you can think of. I had a mental catalog of specs and data points of classic cars that could compete with an encyclopedia. I learned a *ton* about cars—all because I had the passion for them.

As you've seen, that idea carried over into my college education and my business, and it will guide the rest of my life. Passion is what has made me into the man I am today.

We started this book with a discussion of passion, because that's what will make you a valuable team player. Passion will also make you the kind of coach people want to play for. But that's just one of the traits that makes for an excellent leader and coach. In this chapter we'll discuss thirteen more—qualities you can work on right now, no matter where you are in your career. To emphasize their equal importance, I've chosen to organize them alphabetically.

CHARISMA

"Really? A man of your stature on the same plane as me?"

My dad was at it again. It was 2014, and he and I were going to the Grey Cup—the professional Canadian football championship. From a distance, he had spotted the premier of Alberta in the terminal and in typical Dad fashion, he had waltzed up and started chatting away.

"I figured you'd be in a golden jet or some such," my dad said.

"This guy's too much!" the premier replied, almost in tears from laughing.

I was amazed. I always knew my dad was charismatic, but this was a whole other level. After a time, they shook hands and my dad came back. He gave me a wink and held up a piece of paper.

"What do you think of that, Davey?"

It was the premier's phone number. On a whim, my dad made friends with the premier of Alberta. I was speechless.

Charisma is that indefinable, intangible quality that makes you irresistible to others; it's that certain *je ne sais quoi*. Call it snap or a fun-loving attitude, this certain something draws people, and my dad was an expert at it. He knew when to tease and was lighting-fast on his feet—he'd knock you down just to build you up even faster, all in good fun, of course.

Maybe it's just in my genes, but I have that same ability. I easily make myself popular among my peers by utilizing the same charm and pazazz that my father did. That energy I exude causes people to want to be around me, making it all the easier to lead. My girlfriend says guys have "man-crushes" on me. "I'll never have to worry about you, Dave. All your admirers are guys."

At least I know I'm doing things right: employees should not want to avoid their boss.

COMMITMENT

As a leader, you can show commitment in many ways: sacrifices of time and energy to benefit the team and the company, keeping your word, following through on timelines and plans.

You can also display commitment toward your team members, specifically, toward helping them succeed. Here's a perfect example: we hired a new salesperson, and my sales manager was not impressed.

"Dave, he's not the sharpest knife in the drawer," he told me about two weeks after the guy had been hired.

"I don't care. We took him on and now we're gonna train him to work the sales floor."

"The floor?! You can't be serious. He's got the IQ of a doorknob!"

I was getting irked. "He might be young and naive but he's got spunk. I like his attitude. And plus, that kid's loyal."

"*Pfft.* What's that matter if he can't tell a hole in the ground from his a—"

"Let me put it this way: he's staying. And if he doesn't sell 150 cars this year, it'll be on you. Now, get out there and teach him the business."

In the end, this salesman did succeed and eventually became a manager.

Nobody gives a puppy away the first time it has an accident on the rug. We commit to raising and training the pup from the beginning. The same goes in life. Once you begin a project, give it an honest try. Most times, like the puppy, things won't work out right away. So many people I meet today are aloof and "floaty"; they're quick to give up, never knowing what could have been.

All that said, as a rule, give things a little more effort than what you think you ought to. Show commitment.

COMMUNICATE

As a coach, you must know how to communicate. A lack of communication isn't benign; it doesn't mean people merely miss out on information. A lack of communication creates distance and frustration in your team, just as it does with your customers. Everyone reacts the same way when they feel ignored: angry. You can get ahead of these issues by leading and communicating well.

One of the best ways to do this is simply letting people know what's going on. This is why I send out newsletters and have kick-off meetings. When people know what's happening, where they're going, and how we'll get there, they relax; it gives them comfort. I even tell my employees to bring their significant others to the kickoff meetings, and they do! Once a husband or wife hears what's going on at Renfrew they understand why their loved one is working ten hours a day. All around, communication makes for a happier environment.

COMPETENCE

People want to know that their leader knows what he's doing. Not that he's perfect, but that he is competent.

When leaders are given their position on a silver platter, everyone knows it. They quickly pick up on the fact that the person really doesn't know what they're doing. Even if you're still learning your role, like I was when I switched to retail, you still want to show your employees what you do know. And then keep figuring out what you don't.

Like all of these traits, competence is something that can be acquired. With some study and experience and a willingness to learn from your mistakes, you'll be a pro in no time.

COURAGE

I'd be lying if I didn't tell you I was a tad bit nervous when I bought the Renfrew dealership at thirty-four years of age. It was a risk and I had to take a leap of faith, believing I could do it. The same is true when you go to that job interview you feel is *just* out of your league or ask that good-looking guy or gal on a date. You need courage.

Risk is inherently involved in success, and not just on the retail side of life. The higher you move up in a company, the more your job depends on performance, and the larger the target you paint on your back. As in sports, it's not the players who get fired when the team loses the championship; it's the coach. Leaders get the credit, for good or bad.

As a leader, you need courage to make decisions, especially unpopular ones. Think of a referee who has to make the calls they believe are right, knowing that half of the hundred thousand fans in the stands are going to boo him. Not that you should make it your goal to be unpopular, but if everyone likes you, you're probably not leading like you should. If 10 percent of your employees don't approve of your decisions, you're probably doing the right thing.

EXPECTATIONS

Once your expectations are clear, you have to inspect what you expect—in other words, make sure your team is following through. One of the best ways to inspect what you expect is to ask questions you already know the answers to. I might ask, "Hey, what're our sales for the month again?" I already know where we are in sales but I want to see if my director of finance is doing his or her job. This is a subtle way to keep everyone on their toes.

I took the social media class along with my employees because I want to know the answers. I won't be performing the day-to-day tasks for our social media presence, but I still need the basic knowledge to understand what's going on, ask questions, and manage intelligently. Plus, I want to know if my employees know what they are doing. I have my managers take NADA for the same reason: so *they* can ask the questions and know what's happening.

Setting clear expectations with a certainty of follow-through lets your team know you are serious about the business "rules" and that you keep your word. It's also a way to show a little tough love. If my sales manager tells me we have thirty appointments tomorrow, I'll ask what appointments and then follow up with those salespeople, inspecting what I expect. If I find that the number of sales appointments doesn't add up to thirty, my manager and I have ourselves a "come to Jesus" meeting. You can believe he won't ever lie to me again.

EXAMPLE

Leading by example sets a tone that rubs off on the whole team. When you show that you are holding yourself to the same standards—whether it's timeliness or attention to detail or work ethic—everyone else is much more likely to join in. Your example rubs off on your team.

I take special care to lead by example. In no way whatsoever do I want my employees to just do something "because I said so." I expect them to work on Saturdays because I've worked every Saturday for the last twenty-seven years. I can tell them to work late because I worked key-to-key for fifteen years straight. I ask for twelve-hour days because I work thirteen. I don't *tell* my employees, *I show them.*

If you want to retain the respect of your subordinates, you can only expect from them what you expect from yourself. You can't tell a manager to come in on Saturday so you can go golfing with your buddies. Lead by example.

FOCUS

Too often, meetings are held and quickly forgotten, weakening the overall integrity of the business. When I say something, I want people to know, beyond a shadow of a doubt, that it will come to pass. Every month at our kickoff meeting I state our monthly goal. Then, every day after the meeting, I remind my employees what they need to do to achieve the overall goal—I keep them, and myself, focused.

If you lose focus, your goals *will* fall away and be forgotten; it's just human nature. But as a leader, losing focus also creates a dynamic where your employees don't take you seriously. Essentially, you lose their trust, and that's something nearly impossible to regain.

To maintain focus, you need goals: yearly, monthly, weekly, daily. Regularly communicate these goals with your team, as well as the plan for reaching them. Weekly emails or monthly brainstorming meetings are just two ways to keep everyone focused.

MENTOR

Mentorship is, in my opinion, one of the greatest investments you can make—it's an investment in people, not things.

I've already mentioned the mentors who have invested in me over the years: Rick Moore, Steve Philips, Mike Tarp, Ian Speckman, and many others. These men helped me transition to the retail sector; taught me how to manage, motivate, and lead people; showed me how to set goals, increase sales, and buy businesses— and I am eternally grateful. Now I get to do the same thing for others. I invest in and mentor my team at Renfrew, setting them up for success—a win–win scenario. As I set them up to succeed, I get a better team managing my businesses, and we all profit in the long run.

In business, even the smallest changes have massive results. I've taught my managers how to lower expenses and generate more sales. Renfrew Chrysler does $120 million in sales a year, so even if my team cuts expenses by a measly 1 percent, that's another $1.2 million to the bottom line.

Mentoring is like shepherding a flock. As a leader, you pay attention to the whole team so you know who is doing what, who needs praise and who needs correction, who needs training, and who shows promise in terms of becoming a leader themselves.

Some managers "rule with an iron fist," expecting unquestioned obedience and having no desire to pour into their subordinates. I view my employees as mentees. Leadership is your opportunity to help people grow and eventually form their own teams.

PICKING THE RIGHT MENTEES

Once you've reached a leadership position and begin mentoring, you'll want to be selective about your mentees. You only have so much time and energy, so it makes sense to invest both in people who are teachable and want to learn so they can improve. You want to invest in people who want to succeed and win, just like you.

The few guys I'm currently mentoring were easy to pick: they were the passionate ones, eager to learn all about the car business and not so focused on the money. I'd drop hints now and then, and they ate them up. They wanted it.

That said, when one of my mentees started asking about how much money he could make and when he could start expecting big raises, I had to redirect him: "Look, my friend. I love you, but you're on the fence right now. You're caring too much about the money. Do what I say and money will follow." The kid was losing focus on the love of business itself and needed that hard message. Sometimes mentors need to dole out a little tough love as part of the training.

PROBLEM SOLVER

Remember: problems aren't problems; they're challenges. You can even view them as workouts that make you stronger. Life's full of problems—that's what makes it so fun! Reframe your worldview of the hardships of life and face them head-on. Think of each challenge as an opportunity for learning and for making the next problems easier to solve.

Being a strong problem solver makes you nearly irreplaceable. You can become the go-to person in high-stress challenges because people know you remain unruffled no matter what unknowns pop up.

RELATIONSHIP BUILDER

You can't be a leader if you're not a people person. Or maybe I should say, you can't be a true leader, someone people admire and want to follow.

All of business is about building relationships: we get along to go along, plain and simple. My dealership has one of the largest inventories in western Canada. Why? Because I have great rapport with corporate headquarters. I took the time to get to know the inventory managers as people. I asked questions about their personal and professional lives: where they grew up, where they went to school, what they studied, why they chose Chrysler. When it seemed appropriate, I also passed on things I had learned when I was their age working in corporate, and I always told them to ask if there was anything I could do to help. As a result, they know me and like me, and I get support every month, which equals big money for my dealership.

Even more significant, because of my relationships at the head office I receive a small refund from corporate on what I spend for advertising. Sure, if you're a lawyer charging clients $500 an hour you can get away with not developing relationships. But in *real* business, relationships make all the difference.

If you're on the corporate side, take time to develop relationships with the retailers. My friends from my corporate days still call me up from time to time asking if I'll take some number of vehicles in bank, or cars already built by the factory. We'll chat for a bit, I'll ask for a few perks in return for the favor, build the relationship, and make it happen.

RESPONSIBILITY

True leaders take responsibility for not only themselves but also for those under them. They know that when the team fails, it's because of some shortcoming at the top. Being a responsible leader means knowing it's *your* dealership, it's *your* store, it's *your* business. It means you're conscientious in how you spend the company's money: you don't take advantage of the expense account or buy a first-class ticket when you should get business class. It also means you take ownership of setting expectations and providing the training and support that enables your team to meet their individual goals, as well as the team's.

Obviously, others have the responsibility to do their part, and you shouldn't take responsibility or blame when they don't. You can't control if a salesperson drinks all night and doesn't show up to work. You can correct the person, tell him to straighten up, help him set up a routine, and so on, but he still needs to choose to cooperate.

VISION

Leaders have vision. They have goals, for themselves and for their team, and they have a plan to get there (planning precedes performance, remember?).

Once you have a plan, you can reverse engineer that goal to make an actionable strategy. For example, I want to hit $1 billion in sales per year. To do that, I know I'll need to own ten dealerships because each one does sales of about $100 million a year. To acquire ten dealerships, I needed to pay off Renfrew to get more leverage with the banks. By breaking that goal all the way down, I know what parts of my business I need to work on every day to create the revenue to achieve my goals.

Having a vision means being future-minded while staying grounded in the present. Ask yourself where you want your life and career to be in five years, and then work backward. What do you need to do today, tomorrow, next week, next month, next year to achieve that goal? Once you figure out your plan, *stick to it*. As a leader, you'll do the same for your subordinates. Help them set up their own goals and plan of action, so they are looking ten years down the road and knowing the steps they need to take to get there.

In my monthly kickoff meetings, I share my goals for the team, as well as the checkpoints we will all have along the way to make sure we're on track. I hold my employees to the same standards and push them toward the goals I set. I show them what I'm doing for them (e.g., spending $100,000 in marketing) and ask them what they're going to do in turn.

MAKE A PLAN

This chapter presented thirteen qualities of a leader people want to follow. This isn't an exhaustive list but it will definitely get you started.

Now that you've read the descriptions of each, ask yourself a few questions:

- Which five stand out as the most important?
- Which five am I strong in already?
- Which five do I need to work on most?

Now look more closely at the last five, the ones where you are currently weakest. What practical steps can you take right now to improve in these areas? Can you find a course? Read a book? Follow the blog of a leader who speaks on these topics?

There are no shortcuts to being a great leader. If the staircase has ten steps, you can't skip to number five and reach the top. To become a coach people want to play for, you have to put in the work. The good news is that every one of these qualities is learnable. No matter where you are in your career, now is the time to start.

CONCLUSION

DO THE RIGHT THING AND SUCCESS WILL CHASE YOU

The only reason I was given the opportunity to own Renfrew Chrysler was because I had devoted my career—and life—to doing what's right. Mike Tarp gave me full ownership of Renfrew that first day because he knew the type of man that I was: I didn't lie and never cut corners.

Lots of people out there are focused on chasing money, and they'll chase it forever—*and* run over anyone in their way to it. I don't take that approach, but I know some people do. I had some friends, long since discarded, who had to win at everything. You know the type: everything was a competition and they were going to win it.

I believe you should shoot to win 80 percent of the time in life; that's more than enough. People who have to win 100 percent of the time cut corners and steamroll over others. I'd much rather make $1.00 the right way than $1.10 the wrong way.

I've certainly lost money with this philosophy, but it's worth the peace of mind—plus, it's just the right thing to do. Not everything is about me. A lot of my life is meant for other people.

In addition, I see how some of my former friends are doing now—not well. I wish them the best, but a life of selfishness comes with a bitter end. I stand by that ancient principle: it's better to give than to receive. This pays better dividends than winning 100 percent of the time. People like to help those who have helped them.

Because I know it works, I suggest the following philosophy: Don't chase money. Focus on following your passion, working hard, and treating others the way you want to be treated. Nine times out of ten, success and money will have just been a natural consequence. Karma is real; do what's right and the money will follow.

GAME PLAN

We've talked about the importance of planning and the fact that it precedes performance. So, here's a game plan—practical ideas about what to do with the information you just gained from each chapter.

CHAPTER 1: BE A TEAM PLAYER

- Ask yourself: do I have a job or a career? If you answer "job," then chances are you're not working in your passion.
- If you don't currently love what you do, take time to figure out what you do love and then go for it. Passion is a game changer.

CHAPTER 2: ALWAYS BE LEARNING

- Set a goal of learning something new every day, whether it is a skill or a fun fact. Then write it down so you remember it.
- Read a biography on or memoir by someone you consider successful. Take notes on what they did to get there.
- Take a course to learn a new skill or expand your knowledge in a certain area.
- Don't be afraid to ask questions of your supervisor or mentor.

CHAPTER 3: HARD WORK CREATES LUCK

- Sign up for a few networking events: for example, happy hour meetups, trade shows, or career fairs. While there, find people in other industries and talk to them about how they do marketing, sales, and more. Look for ideas you can apply in your own company.
- On a Sunday when your friends are golfing or watching the game, put in some extra effort to get focused for the week. That extra work always pays off.

CHAPTER 4: PLANNING PRECEDES PERFORMANCE

- Take a look around your office. Are files out of place? Do you have an overflowing stack in your inbox? Set aside an hour or two to get organized. Then do the same at home.
- Every night, update your checklist for the next day. That way you're ready to tackle the next day when you wake up, instead of wasting the first hour figuring out what your day's priorities.
- Look at your daily routines. Which ones are helping and which ones are not? How can you adjust your daily routines for better results?
- The next time you experience a bad situation or a roadblock,

look for at least one specific positive aspect: for example, a lesson you can learn to help you next time.

CHAPTER 5: IMPROVING SKILLS THROUGH TRAINING

- How do your communication skills rank among your peers? Where can you improve? Then read a book and/or practice to improve that skillset.
- Evaluate your writing skills, or better yet, have someone else give you some feedback. If you have room for improvement, ask someone who is well written if they will let you read some of their business letters so you can see how they organize their thoughts. You can also have someone proofread your letters.
- Create a mantra or two that you can repeat to yourself every day. If you are not sold on yourself with confidence, your peers will not be either.

CHAPTER 6: BUILD YOUR TEAM

- When it's time to add to your team, consciously look for someone who has strengths where you are weak. If you are a risk-taker, for example, find someone who is more methodical and cautious.
- Sit down and write a list of priorities in terms of character traits for new team members. For example, do you want someone who is a tactical thinker and has a marketing background, or do you want someone who is a strategic thinker and has a finance background, or some other combination?

- Do a personal attitude check: are you generally positive or negative? If the latter, what can you do to shift your outlook?
- Do you have a mentor? If not, look for someone who can help you become a coach people want to play for.

Where you start on this list is completely up to you. Where are you in your career? What do you need to do first to up your game? After you tackle one action item, come back and choose another. Your game plan will be here.

MAKE THE MOST OF YOUR LIFE

You may have heard of the 80/20 rule, but how about the 90/10 rule: 90 percent of the people in life simply get by. They go to work, pay their bills, and have a nice life. The other 10 percent follow their passion. They work hard, make sacrifices, and live far beyond what they could have dreamed.

There is only one person who can pick which group they want to join: you! If you take the steps one at a time and don't skip the process you have in place for success, the benefits will outweigh the challenges along the way.

You only have one life. Crank it. Get all you can out of it. Build a successful business around something you're passionate about, and then use your success to give back and help others. You'll never know what you can achieve until you get out there and go for it.

ACKNOWLEDGMENTS

I want to thank Gail Fay for her support while I was writing this book. Many thanks to the whole publishing team for making the book a reality.

Thank you to Steven MacDonald for being my sounding board.

Thank you to Hannah MacDonald for her feedback on the manuscript.

Many thanks to the Parks family, the Tutschek family, and Uncle Alex for our fun business banter over the years—with many more years to come. I am still working on gaining "the Flex" to keep up with you.

I want to give a huge thank-you to Molly, Doug, Nolan, and Greyson Lamont. You truly keep me motivated for success. I am nothing but proud of our family. Doug, you are like a second dad to me. You are the best of the best.

To Molly's parents, Kathy and Jim Schaeffer, I consider you family, and your support over the years is nothing but spectacular.

ABOUT THE AUTHOR

DAVE LAMONT is the CEO of Renfrew Business Group and president of Renfrew Chrysler, Lloydminster Nissan, and Royalty RV. Since his first job as a district manager, Dave has been passionate about creating opportunity and building successful teams. He studied business administration at the University of Montana and played for Griz Hockey, the university's hockey team. Dave lives in Calgary, Alberta, Canada.

10911175R00067